D1298160

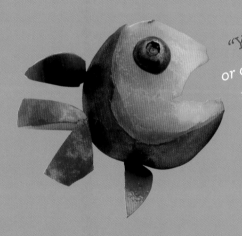

"You don't have to cook fancy or complicated masterpieces—just good food from fresh ingredients." —Julia Child

To Claire, my friend, lover, and muse.

Funny Food

365 Fun, Healthy, Silly, Creative Breakfasts

by Bill & Claire Wurtzel

Edited by Katrina Fried
Designed by Kristen Sasamoto

Welcome Books · New York

Acknowledgments

Thank you to Lisa and Nina, our daughters who willingly put up with my crafty way of getting them to eat well. They were the first children for whom I made funny food. • Special thanks to Nina, for her work on the project. I'm grateful that our grandchildren Ethan, Simon, and Daniela love the silliness and healthy food. • Many friends and family members inspired me and helped make this book possible. I am grateful to them all. • Thanks to Susan McClanahan and Kathleen Cushman, who had the vision of the breakfasts as a book. • Thanks to Howard Morgan for insisting that I follow through, and Ron Green for the creative possibilities he saw in the images. • I would like to acknowledge Morty Metz for contacting Sam Roberts, of the *New York Times*, who wrote a story about the breakfasts and was the first to show them in print. • I am especially appreciative of Sanda Balaban, a constant supporter. • Claire and I wish to thank Lena Tabori, Katrina Fried, and Kristen Sasamoto, our publishing team, for their artistic sensibilities. • Thank you to Alexa Van de Walle for connecting us to Welcome Books and for her ongoing support.

  This book honors the memory of my mother, father, and sister, who always encouraged my artistic pursuits; and my mother-in-law, whose irreverence instilled Claire's sense of joy.

—B.W.

Published in 2012 by Welcome Books®
An imprint of Welcome Enterprises, Inc.
6 West 18th Street, New York, NY 10011
(212) 989-3200; Fax (212) 989-3205
www.welcomebooks.com

Publisher: Lena Tabori
Editor: Katrina Fried
Designer: Kristen Sasamoto

Copyright © 2012 Welcome Enterprises, Inc.
Photographs copyright © 2012 Bill Wurtzel

For further information about this book please visit: www.welcomebooks.com/funnyfood

Library of Congress Cataloging-in-Publication data on file.

ISBN: 978-1-59962-111-1
First Edition
10 9 8 7 6 5 4 3 2 1
Printed in China

Table of Contents

Introduction

I met Bill at a dance the summer of 1960. His laugh and sense of humor instantly captured my heart. Bill was an advertising art director and he made playful food to make me laugh even then.

Bill has continued to create fun breakfasts for me over the past fifty years. He is not a trained cook by any means, but he can turn any combination of ingredients into a feast for the eyes. "I saw the angel in the marble and carved until I set him free," Michelangelo once said. That is the way Bill creates his food art, too. He looks at a slice of melon or some fried eggs, and sees something that no one else would see—a head, an arm, the wheels of a bicycle, the wings of a butterfly—waiting to be discovered.

Bill's sense of whimsy reminds me of my mother. When I was a child, she baked challah bread every Friday. She always gave me my own little piece of extra dough to shape, while she fashioned funny objects like little birds, or tiny braided breads. My favorite was the dirty feet she made with cinnamon and raisins between the toes. Bill's endless capacity to create artistic breakfasts that I devour in mere minutes has been a wonderful gift throughout our marriage, and a constant reminder of my childhood joy.

Because I have been a "Weight Watcher" for many years, Bill has always been mindful to create breakfasts for me that are high in flavor and nutrition, and low in calories and fat. My fanciful breakfasts make me slow down, focus on what's on my plate, and eat less.

When our daughters, Lisa and Nina, were young children, Bill made eating healthy meals fun for them too, through food play and telling imaginary stories about the food on their plates. We saw how responsive our own children—and, later, grandchildren—were to this creative approach, and realized it could be a wonderful tool to encourage child nutrition.

Armed with hundreds of Bill's brilliant breakfast photos, and my background as an educator, we initiated Funny Food workshops for school-age kids to promote healthy eating habits. We explain the importance of combining food groups and demonstrate this by making a breakfast with the children's input. They gain insight into an artist's eye and an understanding of how food nurtures their bodies and minds. They are focused, excited, and love making their own fantasies come to life on the plate. The best part is watching the children gobble up their delicious creations. Studies show that children remember content when lessons are hands-on and taught in a joyful atmosphere, and our workshop experiences confirm this to be true.

It's a joy and an act of love to start the day with an artistic, healthy breakfast. Bill, an artist and jazz musician, considers these dishes as fleeting improvisations—moments of pleasure that are to be consumed and disappear like the Mandala sand paintings of the Tibetan Lamas. Photographing his work has enabled us, and our friends and family, to enjoy his edible masterpieces long after the plates have been licked clean, and now it is our great pleasure to extend that delight and inspiration to all of you.

—Claire Wurtzel

Tips for Making Funny Food

◼ **WACKY IS GOOD** The imaginations of children are boundless, and allowing them to create without imposing judgments is essential to their development. They may see odd things in the shape of a piece of cheese or an egg that you could never have fathomed. Give them the positive reinforcement they need to let their imaginations run wild.

◼ **IT'S A BALANCING ACT** Balance is the key word. Combining various food groups is the heart of good nutrition. An assortment of foods on the plate is also a natural way to teach portion control. Instead of three pancakes, one pancake and some fruit and protein provide a more balanced mixture of needed nutrients with a healthy amount of calories, fat, and sugar.

◼ **KEEP IT ALL IN THE FAMILY** When families share mealtimes, children are less likely to snack on unhealthy foods. Providing wholesome ingredients for them to choose from and eating their creations together is emotionally satisfying, fun, and teaches children about nutrition.

◼ **LAY IT ALL OUT** Have the ingredients set out and ready to work with. Buy a variety of healthy ingredients that will make good images and add diversity to the child's diet.

◼ **TOOLS OF THE TRADE** The tools you will need include a cutting board, a knife for you, and a plastic knife for the child if she/he is ready for it. Having fun with a creative food activity might make the child want to try using a new utensil, like a whisk or a melon baller. Encourage the child to do as much as he/she would like. These first steps build independence, which children of all ages crave, and adds to their investment in eating what they have created.

■ KEEP IT CLEAN Be sure to wash your hands and your child's hands before handling any food. Fruits and vegetables should also be washed thoroughly under water to remove any film of dirt or pesticides.

■ FOLLOW THE LEADER Some children have sensory issues and are uncomfortable feeling and tasting certain textures. Respect their wishes and let them observe you touch and play with the food. They may eventually want to have the hands-on experience, too. With younger children, try to think out loud so they hear you plan the process of creating your plate of art, and explain the steps involved. Learning about sequences is an important part of school and life.

■ SEEING IS BELIEVING The way food looks goes a long way toward encouraging children to eat something they haven't tried before. Eating habits are formed during these childhood years and if healthy foods are introduced early in a fun way, they will learn to make good choices on their own.

■ RULES OF ENGAGEMENT Teach your children when it's appropriate to play with their food and when it is not—like when they're at restaurants or visiting other people's homes. If you are consistent and clear about the rules of food play, your children will accept those rules naturally.

■ TAKE YOUR TIME Making an artistic creation takes time. Try starting this on weekends when there is time to look at and examine new foods. If the food is created and presented in a joyful manner, the child will remember the food, the nutrition it provides, and the playful experience.

The Good Egg

Scrambled, poached, hard-boiled, soft-boiled, fried, or in an omelet, frittata, or quiche, eggs are a healthy way to start the day. Contrary to previous beliefs, new research shows that moderate consumption of eggs does not have a negative impact on cholesterol. If you're otherwise eating a well-balanced, low fat/cholesterol diet, then eggs are a great daily source of protein, essential amino acids, and nutrients. And don't skip the yolks—they contain most of the egg's vitamin supply.

Eggs are *versatile,* easy to cook, affordable, delicious & highly *nutritious.*

fry it!

In a sauté pan over medium-low heat, melt a small pat of butter.
Once butter has completely melted, crack eggs into pan. Reduce
heat to low and cover for a minute or two. Once the whites have
completely set, remove eggs from pan and serve.

step one

step two

step three

step four

It's as easy as 1·2·3·4!

15

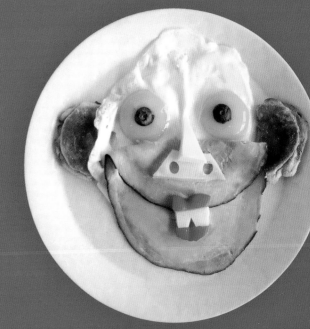

Free Birds!

When possible, always opt for *organic free range* eggs.

They're higher in omega-3 fatty acids, are free of antibiotic and pesticide residues, and contain no arsenic, which is added to factory-farmed chicken-feed to prevent infections and accelerate growth.

scramble *it!*

The real secret to making the creamiest, most perfect scrambled eggs is slow cooking. Whisk desired number of eggs until they are completely smooth and uniform in color. Season with salt and pepper to taste and add a dash of milk. In a non-stick sauté pan over low heat, melt a small pat of butter. Add whisked eggs to pan and stir slowly with a wooden spoon until eggs are cooked through, but still creamy.

Keep it Fresh!

Parsley is a good source of vitamin A, vitamin C, vitamin K, iron, and folate, and is great for heart health.

Basil is packed with vitamin K, iron, calcium, and vitamin A, and is a natural anti-inflammatory.

For the best flavor and highest nutritional value, try to use fresh organic herbs instead of dried.

Have Fun with Funghi! Mushrooms are fat-free, cholesterol-free, and packed with nutrition. In fact, one medium-sized portobello has as much potassium as a banana. Potassium is an essential mineral, one that helps our heart, bones, and muscles grow and function at their very best.

Bakin' Bacon!

A little lower in saturated fat and calories than pork bacon, turkey bacon is a healthier way to get your bacon fix. To keep it guilt-free—choose brands that are low in sodium, and bake instead of frying.

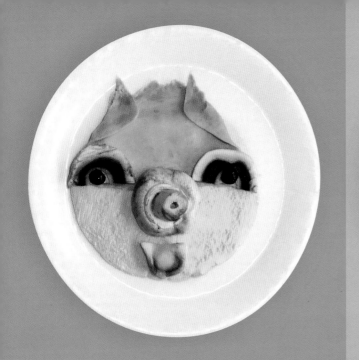

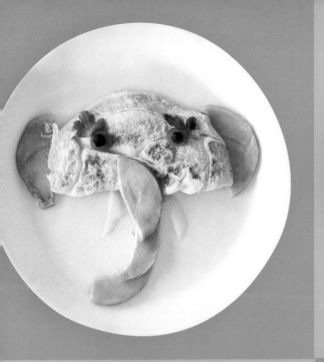

boil it!

Remove eggs from refrigerator and leave sitting out for an hour or until they've reached room temperature. Fill a pot with water, high enough to submerge eggs by about an inch. Place desired number of eggs in water and bring to a boil over medium-high heat. Cover the pot and remove from heat. For a soft cooked yolk, let sit for 4 to 5 minutes. For a medium cooked yolk, 6 to 7 minutes. And for a hard cooked yolk, 15 to 18 minutes.

Whole grain breads are a great source of vitamins, magnesium, iron & fiber—a natural aid to healthy digestion.

Always read the label—many so-called "wheat breads" are made with refined flour, which is not nearly as nutritionally rich.

57

Whole wheat *and* whole grain **waffles and pancake** make a healthy high fiber canvas for a nutritious **masterpiece...**

Add some vitamin-rich berries or a few protein-packed nuts to create a face that fits your mood. Blueberry and cottage cheese eyes, banana ears, bacon eyebrows—the possibilities are endless....

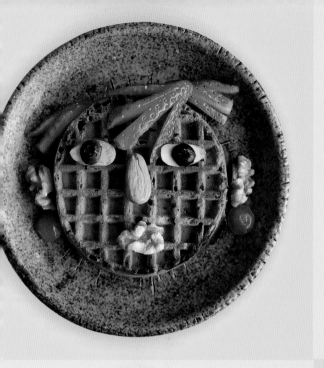

Whole wheat pancakes are a snap to whip up from scratch, and can be made in an endless number of fun shapes and sizes.

Whole wheat pancakes

1 cup whole wheat flour

1 tsp baking powder

½ tsp baking soda or substitute
    baking powder

⅛ tsp salt

1 egg, lightly beaten

1 cup low-fat buttermilk

2 tbsp honey

To make the batter, whisk whole wheat flour, baking powder, baking soda and salt in a medium bowl. In a small bowl, combine egg, buttermilk and honey. Make a well in dry ingredients and stir in egg and buttermilk mixture. Allow batter to rest for a few minutes. Preheat griddle to 375 degrees or set a nonstick frying pan to medium-high heat. Drop batter by ¼ cupfuls on to griddle or pan. Cook until the edges begin to dry and bubbles appear in the pancakes. Flip and cook for 1–2 minutes more.

Makes 8 pancakes.

A steamy bowl of oatmeal with some fruit and nuts is one of the healthiest ways you can start the day.

Steel It!

Nutty and rustic, the only drawback to making steel cut oats instead of rolled oats is their longer cooking time. You can get around this by starting the night before. Bring four cups of water to boil in a medium pot, add one cup of oats and a teaspoon of salt, and return to a boil. Turn off the heat, cover, and let sit on the stove overnight. In the morning, heat the oatmeal and simmer until tender, about 15 to 20 minutes. Stir in a half a cup of low-fat or fat-free milk for some added protein and creaminess. Add toppings of fruit, nuts, and raisins for a well-balanced breakfast. Serves 4.

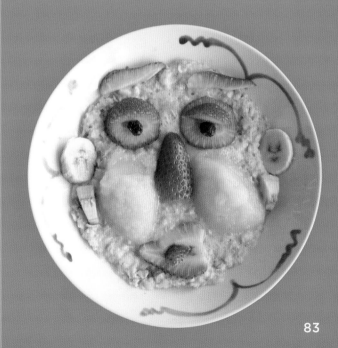

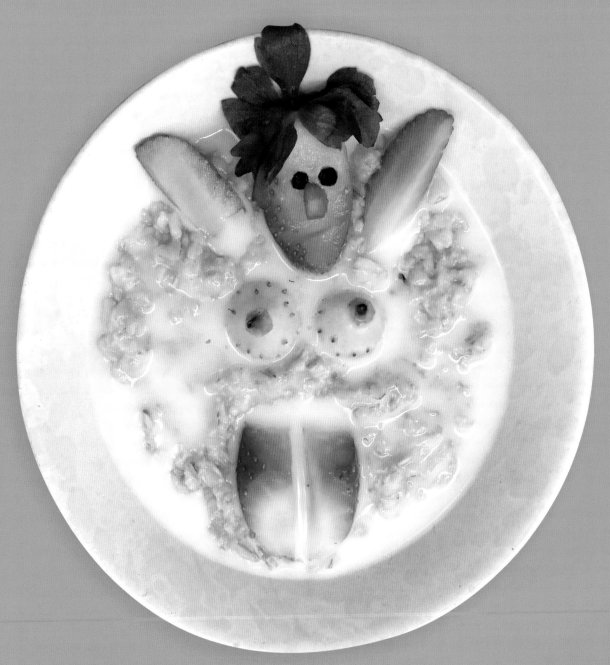

All cereals are not created equal! Look for whole grain cereals made from wheat or bran—like shredded wheat or bran flakes—and avoid anything made with extra sugar or refined flour. Add some low-fat milk and vitamin-rich berries for sweetness!

Eat me!

Whole grain cereals are a good source of soluble fiber, which acts almost like a little sponge, sucking up bad cholesterol in your body, and they contain even more insoluble fiber, which helps maintain healthy digestion.

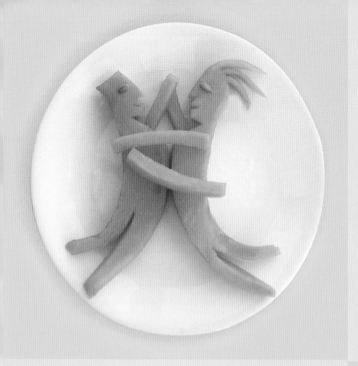

By filling your plate with a **rainbow** *of produce,*

you are guaranteed a diverse sampling of essential vitamins and minerals.

The color of a fruit or vegetables is a small clue to its range of vitamins and nutrients.

before...

after!

Don't Skip the Peel!

Nearly half of the vitamin C found in an apple is located in the flesh just beneath the skin—which also contains valuable amounts of insoluble fiber.

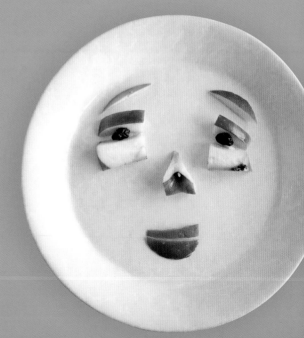

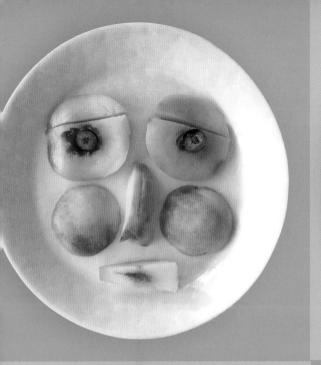

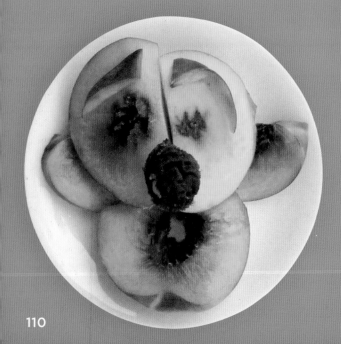

The bigger the navel,
the sweeter the orange!

Navel oranges are the most popular kind of orange to eat. They're easy to peel, sweet, and seedless. Named after the belly-button shape at one end of the stem, they're bursting with vitamin C, fiber, and other antioxidants.

Whole wheat *pitas* are low in fat, high in *fiber*, and fun to stuff with your favorite foods. Plus, they make *great faces!*

The pocket in a pita is made by steam, which puffs up the dough while it's cooking. As the pita cools and flattens, a pocket is left in the middle.

YO-YO for **yogurt!**

Yogurt is curdled milk with **added live cultures,** which help **stave off** bacteria.

Though cow's milk is the most common type of yogurt, it can be made from the milk of any mammal—in some countries they eat camel milk yogurt!

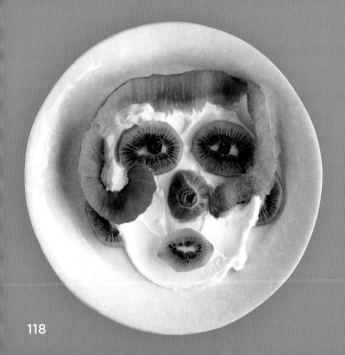

berry *delicious!*

Ounce for ounce, strawberries have as much vitamin C as oranges. Just one cup of raw strawberries delivers 160% of the recommended daily dose of Vitamin C.

Did you know? Folklore has it that if you split a double strawberry with someone, it will make him or her fall in love with you.....Strawberries were once called "heart-seed berries" by Native Americans—who pounded them into cornmeal bread.

122

step one

step two

step three

step four

It's as easy as 1·2·3·4!

127

The Lucky Peach!

In China, the peach is a symbol of longevity and good fortune. Maybe that's because they're filled with health-promoting nutrients, like vitamin A, vitamin C, dietary fiber, and potassium.

Go Nuts!

Packed with protein, fiber, vitamin E, and a bevy of other vitamins and minerals, nuts are little nuggets of nutrition and energy. Eating a handful a day can also help lower cholesterol and the risk of heart disease.

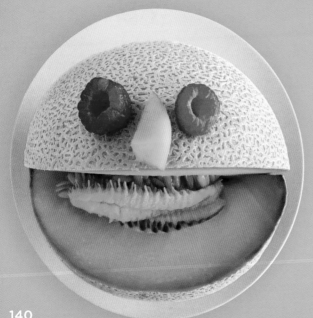

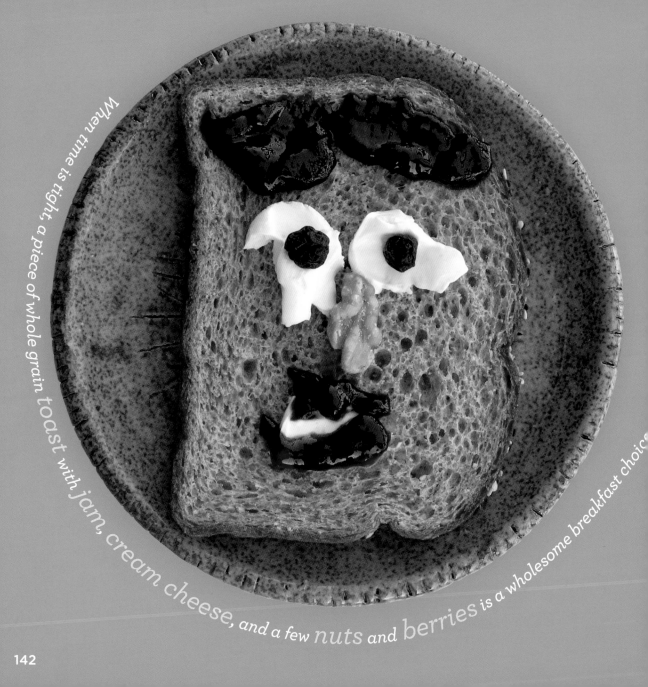

When time is tight, a piece of whole grain *toast* with jam, *cream cheese*, and a few *nuts* and *berries* is a wholesome breakfast choice

To keep the fat and sugar down, look for low-fat cream cheese or just use a small amount, and buy jam or fruit spread that has no added sugar.

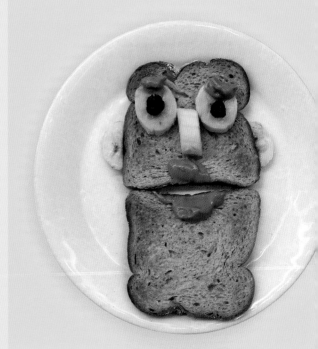

Better than Butter!

Rich in protein, niacin, and folate, kid-favorite peanut butter is a healthy way to *kick start your day.*

Did you know....? The peanut is not a nut but a legume, related to the bean and lentil... Arachibutyrophobia is the fear of peanut butter sticking to the roof of your mouth.

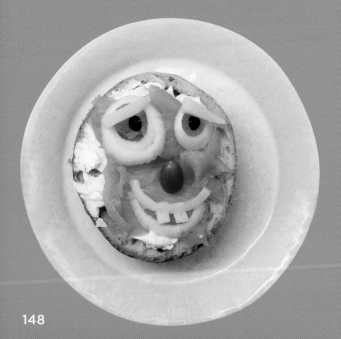

Smoked salmon and cream cheese is not just a tasty classic breakfast combination—it's also good for you!

Salmon is low in cholesterol, calories, and saturated fat, but high in omega-3 fat, which can have a slew of positive effects on the body—from lowering blood pressure and the risk of heart disease, to fighting depression.

Always opt for wild-caught salmon when you can—it's better for the envi-ronment and better for your body! Wild-caught has fewer pesticides and antibiotics, more bioavailable omega-3, and no artificial coloring.

Nuts, fruits, veggies, whole grains, and proteins—like tuna, cheese, and hummus—are all great components for a a wholesome snack.

For a protein-rich *pop* of energy a *slice* or two of deli meat can work like a *charm*.

Turn a slice of turkey, ham, or cheese into the base for your face, and use some veggies, mustard, pickles, olives, or salad to add on the features. Look for low-sodium, low-fat cold cuts, and always buy organic!

And of course, don't forget to eat your veggies!